MW00881747

"No Nursing Home for Me!"
By G. Keith Murphy

Elder Law Attorney and Estate Planner

ISBN

"I Sang Danny Boy At The Nursing Home The Other Day

There Wasn't A Dry Seat In The House."

ACKNOWLEDGMENT AND DEDICATION

Fifteen years ago, my mother died all alone in a small room in a nursing home. She had been in a drug-induced, semi-conscious state for months prior to her death. For all practical purposes, she had been dead for weeks when her heart beat its last beat. As much as I loved my mother, I found myself wanting the end to come sooner, rather than later, because I knew that would be her wish as well.

You would not be reading this Guide, but for my mother, Vera Murphy. She was the one who insisted that I get involved in 4-H demonstrations when I was in the 5th grade at Funston school. She helped me write my 4-H speeches, and she instilled in me at 11 years of age, the confidence and poise I needed to speak in front of groups of people. With her support, I won every school, district, and state public speaking competition I ever entered (except one notable exception). I will never forget those 4-H demonstrations, especially the two which got me started on my way: "How to Control Hornflies on Beef Cattle" and "Cotton, and it's Many Uses".

Because of her continuous encouragement and un-limited faith in me, my confidence and skill-set grew. I won the FFA public speaking contest when I was in the 11th grade in high school, competing against all other FFA members, including upperclassmen. Our chapter was the largest FFA chapter in the world at that time.

In 1973, my Mercer teammate and I were voted "Best Oralists" in Interstate Moot Court competition against teams from other law schools across the Southeastern United States. Additionally, I have argued in front of the Supreme Court of Georgia, and I once convinced a jury to spare a cop-killer's life; it was my job to do so.

My mother was the sweetest woman who ever lived (other than your mother), and I dedicate this Guide to her honor and memory. During her lifetime, she enhanced the quality of life for everyone who knew her . . . she made life better. That is the intent of my Guide, hopefully, to offer suggestions and options for making life a little better, even during its end stages.

ABOUT THE AUTHOR

One of the first classes Keith attended at Mercer University in 1966, was Professor Brewster's Christianity class; Christianity was a required course at this private, Baptist University. As professor Brewster started the course, Keith expected the usual lecture he had heard all of his life, that a Christian should accept "on faith" all the things he didn't understand. Keith was shocked at what he heard that morning.

"If your Christian beliefs cannot withstand your scrutiny, it does not deserve your devotion" is the way Keith remembers the lesson that day.

Keith was 18 then, and he is now 73, but he still rarely accepts without question the status quo, the traditional, the "tried and true" way of doing anything. His adventuresome curiosity has backfired on him occasionally.

Roscoe Gay, a long-time family friend, once said, "If you're not making a mistake from time to time, then you must not be going forward."

It is this Keith Murphy, the man who questions the obvious, probes the perimeters of conventional wisdom, and experiments with new ideas, who presents this Guide for your consideration. You won't find any far-flung notions, but the ideas presented, in military lingo, are clearly walking point.

In addition to being a long-time lawyer, Keith has published two memoirs, "Whoa Yonder!" and "Tomfoolery and Tragedy", a historical fiction novel, "Where Long Beards Grow", and a collection of short stories, "Stories from a Route Four Man". All are available on Amazon.

PREFACE

My grandmother died in a nursing home when I was a young man; I didn't visit her very often, because she was always asleep. My grandfather also died while living his last few years in a nursing home. He was doing well, the checker champion at age 95, but he was given the wrong medicine, and never recovered.

The nursing home blamed the outside pharmacy, and the pharmacy claimed the nursing home staff had given Granddaddy another patient's medicine. We never learned the truth; Granddaddy was just as dead either way.

In December, 2019, I spent a week in a nursing home recovering from open heart surgery. I was only 71 years old, and although I was physically weak, my mind was alert, and I was fully aware of the quality of care I was receiving. I was no "shrinking violet" when it came to expressing my displeasure with my treatment. Moreover, I was a fairly well-known attorney in town, not someone that staff would single-out to neglect or mistreat. If anything, I anticipated the best of care, especially since I had a large Facebook following to whom I reported daily. Even with all of these things going for me, my week in the nursing home was the most dehumanizing event of my life.

It is not my intent to rant, page after page, about the way I was treated, or the way others have been treated in nursing homes. In fact, I believe there are thousands of skilled caregivers and support staff across this nation who daily provide dignified and necessary services to nursing home residents; I choose to believe that, whether it's true or not.

Yet, I compare the loss of my mother and grandparents with the death of my father. Roy Murphy died in his bed at home, surrounded by his wife and children, and with a houseful of relatives, friends and neighbors who were there to show their love and respect. He was able to communicate up until the last few hours of his life. He knew we were with him, loving him, and holding his hand when he took his last breath. That was over 40 years ago.

I know we cannot turn back the clock to a gentler time, yet there is no excuse for us to continue to travel the road we are on. If you find dying in a nursing home to be as repugnant as I do, then stay tuned.

CONTENTS

Section One. Avoiding The Nursing Home

Chapter One. What's all the fuss about?
Chapter Two. Rich man walking here, boss!
Chapter Three. "What you talkin' about Lewis?"
Chapter Four. Smoke and Mirrors
Chapter Five. Let's all Dance.
Chapter Six. Will the best insurance plan please stand up?
In Conclusion

Section Two. End Of Life Options

Chapter Seven. Elvis has left the Building. Maybe not.
Chapter Eight. "I know my Rights . . . ."
Chapter Nine. This is not Rocket Science.
Chapter Ten. Eli's Coming!
In Conclusion

SECTION ONE

Avoiding the Nursing home

CHAPTER ONE

What's all the fuss about?

Here is where I can bore you to death with statistics, and that's not what I want to do. We all know there are:

a) tons of old people shuffling around out there already; and

b) more old people are coming down the pike than ever before; and

c) old people get sick, and are often unable to care for themselves; and

d) a nursing home is the default setting for warehousing severely disabled senior citizens.

No statistics needed, right? But now, looky here; the perfect storm is developing, and it's just over the horizon. Here are some indicators:

A. *Baby Boomers*.

Blame it on the baby boomers, but the number of seniors 65 years and older is expected to almost double over the next 40 years.

"Forty years, my Lord, who cares what happens 40 years from now?"

I suggest to you that the 40-, 50-, and 60-year-olds of today should be very concerned about what will be happening in the next 20, 30 and 40 years.

B. *Living Longer.*

Americans have gained almost 10 years of life expectancy over the last 50 plus years. Average life expectancy has increased from 69.9 in 1959 to 78.9 in 2014.

Statistics indicate the older a person becomes, the greater the chance he will need long term care. Almost 70 percent of seniors 65 and over will need some form of long-term care.

What we have so far, is more old folks than ever before, living longer than ever before, and needing more long-term care than ever before. That can't be good, but there's more bad news.

C. *Dementia, the long goodbye, is enemy number One for seniors.*

There is no known cure for dementia, and its victim gets progressively worse over time. The average life expectancy for someone diagnosed with Alzheimer's is 10 years, but can vary greatly with some patients living 20 years or longer.

Dementia will take away a person's ability to live independently about as quickly as anything you can imagine. At the present time, there are 6 million Americans living with Alzheimer's, but by 2050, a short 30 years from now, that number is expected to be nearly 13 million.

While medical science seems to be making good progress against some ailments, such as heart disease, little progress is being made to get dementia under control. For example, between 2000 and 2019, deaths from heart disease have decreased 7.3 percent while deaths from Alzheimer's have INCREASED 145 percent!

D. "Houston, we have a problem."

The purpose of the statistics above is to show the mad scramble that seniors will likely be facing in the near future as old age, bad health, record-breaking demand for care services, and limited resources, all collide, probably within our lifetime. This Guide was not written to solve the problems facing America and most other countries of the world, but rather, is intended to RALLY YOU, and to help guide you towards developing your own "bug-out" bag, i.e., old-age plan.

Please don't tell me you plan to live at home with your loving family taking care of you. That will hold true for a lucky few, but many seniors are already living at home alone, and those numbers are expected to increase.

Statistics show that 26 percent of all women aged 65 to 74 are already living at home alone; 39 percent of women from 75 to 84 live alone, and 55 percent of women over 85 are living alone.

If you can't get family members to live with you now, why do you think they will move in and take care of you when you are old, irritable, sick, helpless, and half out of your mind? I can barely get a birthday card out of my family members as it is, and I doubt that any of them are going to pause their lives and move in to become my caretaker.

Heaven forbid, I should have to move into their bee hive.

As one of my mentors often said, "It's time to wake up and smell the coffee!" The cold hard truth is, if you live as long as you want, you will almost certainly lose the ability to live independently.

Sure, you may be one of the lucky ones who enjoys good health until you're 95, and die while in your easy chair half-way thru an episode of "Ironside." But as our new President says, "Come on, man... here's the real deal," millions of us will end up needing long term care.

Far too many of us will not be able to do two or more of the six essential activities of daily living {ADL's): Bathing, Dressing, Eating, Transferring, (moving from bed to wheelchair and back again), Toileting (the ability to get on and off the toilet by yourself), and Continence (ability to control your bladder and bowel functions).

If you can't do two of the six things described above, you have officially met Medicaid's definition for being "medically-qualified" for nursing home care. That same criteria is used to qualify for benefits under most long-term care insurance policies.

The purpose of this Guide is to **EDUCATE, MOTIVATE**, and **FACILITATE.**

a) To educate the reader both as to the harsh realities of old age and death, and the options which are available to confront both; and
b) To motivate our seniors to PLAN now, and to ACT now, while they are still healthy and alert; and
c) To facilitate those who wish to live and die on their own terms.

If you're with me, follow me.

"I want to die peacefully in my sleep, like my grand-father.

Not screaming and yelling like the passengers in his car."

CHAPTER TWO

"Rich man walking here, boss!"

While we are being straight-up with each other, there are a couple of more things I need to disclose at this juncture. Some of you don't need the nuts and bolts I offer in later chapters in order to build your personal old age plan.

As my Uncle used to say, some of *you are "as rich as 4 foot up a bull's ass",* and you have the financial means to pay for excellent at-home care indefinitely, or at least until your clock stops ticking. The least of your worries is dying in a crowded, public nursing home. You don't need Medicaid, Long Term Care Insurance, or to marry some rich old widow woman.

For you, I would suggest skipping some of the following chapters, and moving on to the section that deals with "End of Life Options." No matter how much money you have, you're going to die one day, and you will be surprised at how much control you may have over that process. There are some things you need to know, and some plans you might wish to make.

But before you fat-cats go, stick around for a few more pages.

To some degree, the quality of life you enjoy in your old age, depends on how much money you have to throw at the problem. Those with deep pockets can afford to devise their own long term care plan. You can choose to live in a luxurious home, and have the best doctors, nurses, caregivers, and waitstaff that money can buy.

The fact that you can do it, however, is still a step or two away from ACTUALLY doing it. It's like the little boy said, "I can lift two hundred pounds over my head anytime I want to!" He just never wanted to.

For you, I see my job as motivating you to get off your keyster. My first piece of advice is to SPEND some of that money! And then, SPEND some more! What higher purpose can your money ever serve than to enhance the quality of your life during your final years on this Earth?

I recall the story of a fabulously wealthy man who, when approached by the Grim Reaper, tried to negotiate a little bit more time. The man offered half of his tremendous wealth to the Reaper, if he would be allowed another 30 days of life. The Reaper rejected his offer, and the man offered a larger portion of his wealth for just one additional week. The last offer was all of his wealth for just another hour.

One more word to the well-heeled: yes, your money can be used to buy the best, but the "best" in whose opinion? If you suffer a sudden stroke with resulting dementia, someone, perhaps a spouse or an agent operating under an enhanced Power of Attorney, will use your money to design the care you are to receive for the rest of your life. The plan they come up with may not be to your liking, but at that stage of the game, there may be little you can do about it.

Who picks out the shoes which you wear every day, or

the car you choose to drive, or the food you will eat when you visit that Italian restaurant down the street? But now you tell me, you're going to let someone else decide how, where, and under what conditions you will live out your final years?

Good grief!

Would you prefer to spend your last days in a small, luxurious personal care home in sunny Florida, or in a high-rise convalescent center in Detroit? Perhaps, move closer to your only child and grandchildren in Denver, or stay near your boyhood home in New Hampshire? Big city or nature's wonderland?

After all, without a plan, the person you entrust to 'look after you' may cut some corners to preserve their inheritance. If you've ridden in the front seat all of your life, now is not the time to be put in the rear of the bus.

If you've been frugal, perhaps too frugal, now may be the time to soak up a little extravagance, and enjoy a little pampering. You need it more now than ever before, and it's your last chance to be good to yourself. Quit denying yourself!

As one of my ex-wives frequently said, "You always have a choice!" You can afford this last vacation, and YOU should be the one deciding where you're going, and how you're going to get there. Make your plan while you are healthy; buy that nice retirement condo on the beach near world-famous Shands Hospital. Where is the best place you have ever lived, the place that holds your fondest memories? What are you waiting for? **By golly, do something, dammit!**

At age 52, I made the decision to take early retirement from the practice of law. I had been up to my eyeballs in law for 30 years at that point, and I needed a break. I had lived in Moultrie, Georgia, all of my life, and I needed a change of scenery. I retired and moved to the beautiful mountains of North Georgia, the best decision I ever made in my life.

Every day, I would be tending to my 7 acres, sawing logs, cutting firewood, mowing the pastures, caring for my horses, taking long mountain rides through the adjoining, government-owned forests, just enjoying every moment of my life.

At the end of the private road we lived on, was another retired lawyer. Ed had retired at age 79, and moved to the mountains with his wife. Both Ed and Marilyn had health issues which prevented them from being very active. Ed loved horses, and owned a couple, but it was a struggle just to care for them. Neither he nor Marilyn were able to ride, or go for mountain hikes, or do anything physically challenging.

Ed and I became friends, and one day, as he watched me do my chores at my horse barn, he commented, "I just waited too late . . . too late".

Ed was witnessing exactly what he had missed in life, by refusing to follow his dreams until he was too old and in poor health.

I took a 20-year break, a super-active retirement, most days chasing after my dreams. Eventually, life brought me back to my hometown to live out my old age on the family farm, and to re-engage the community as an Elder Law attorney. I couldn't be happier with the choices I made.

I tell this personal history to underscore the fact that choices do exist, especially for people with financial means. Whoever heard of a lawyer retiring at age 52, and reactivating his license, and going back to work at age 72? You must be brave and bold to take the less-traveled roads. To break from a riptide, you must act counter-intuitively, by not swimming towards the shore, but swimming parallel to the shore.

Who says you must grow old, become disabled, move into a nursing home, and die there after vegetating yourself into eternity? Break away from the riptide of conventional wisdom before it drowns you!

The one thing, perhaps the only thing, I ever taught my two oldest granddaughters, was:

"Skylar, Savannah, who is going to take care of you if you don't take care of yourself?"

"NOBODY, Granddaddy!"

Getting back on subject, everyone knows about assisted living homes which usually are much more desirable and less expensive than nursing homes, but few people know about Continuing Care Retirement Communities (CCRC's).

CCCR's are developments which provide living arrangements for elders with a built-in continuum of care. The senior can move in when he is healthy and fully capable of living independently, and as his health fails, the CCCR has programs which will provide any level of care required for the remainder of his life.

These developments are "one and done" facilities, sometimes called "aging in place," because you arrive in good health, and your care in the community can be adjusted to meet your needs as you grow older and more dependent.

Just like motels, from the Super Eight to the Ritz Carlton, the standard of living, and the cost to join such a community, can vary tremendously. There is a website that lists most of the accredited CCRC's throughout the United States, and there you can find links to connect with individual websites to get the low-low on each facility. **https://www.caring.com/senior-living/continuing-care-retirement-communities/**

For example, there are 14 CCRC's listed in Georgia. Check out the "Marshes at Skidway Island," where you might think you have died and gone to heaven, as opposed to moving into an old-age community.

Finally, there are people who actually make a career of helping old folks make appropriate choices; they are called "geriatric care managers." These people are to seniors planning their end-game, what realtors are to house-hunters. If you are at the age where it takes you 30 minutes to find your car in the parking lot, you might need a little professional help. Check out **www.aginglifecare.org** to locate people in the know.

In conclusion, for those of you who do not need government assistance in your final years, there is no excuse for you not having a plan. It is a buyer's market, a virtual smorgasbord of options. All you have to do is to decide to spend some of that money, and there are plenty of people around who are willing to help you do that.

Morris, an 82 year-old man, went to the doctor to

get a physical. A few days later the doctor saw Morris walking down the street with a gorgeous young woman on his arm.

A couple of days later the doctor spoke to Morris and said, "You're really doing great, aren't you?"

Morris replied, "Just doing what you said, Doc: 'Get a hot mamma and be cheerful.'

"The doctor said, "I didn't say that. I said, 'You've got a heart murmur. Be careful.'"

CHAPTER THREE

What you talking 'bout, Lewis?

Some of you may be a little confused; Arnold from "Diff'rent Strokes" comes to mind. And that's what I am talking about, different strokes for different folks.

Let's face it; time to stop and smell the coffee. There are people who have little to no money, and who have no family or friends who are able or willing to take them in. It would seem those seniors have no choices; they are nursing home bound if they medically-qualify. The only bright spot is, people with no financial means have no trouble getting financially-qualified for Medicaid.

"How do they manage to stay out of a nursing home? Do they have no options?" you ask.

Well, not exactly. Their options may be more limited, but there are things which can be done.

While I will give you a suggestion or two in the next Chapter about securing government assistance when you're old and disabled, that option should be considered only after you have worn out your brain trying to devise a workable plan.

A buddy of mine had a saying, "Two heads are always better than one, even if one is a pumpkin head!"

So, starting with the basics, we are talking about getting some assistance when you are no longer able to care for yourself. That "assistance" comes in two flavors: paid-for assistance and free-assistance. We've already established that you are broke, so, initially, we're shopping down the "free-assistance" aisle.

One thing to bear in mind, there are a lot of people who are in the same boat with you. I hear the cries of our forefathers, "United we stand, divided we fall," "Strength in numbers," "I'll scratch your back, if you'll scratch mine," or in the immortal words of Roy D. Mercer, *"Wait 'til my brother gets off work, and me and him's gonna whip your ass!"*

The point is, what you can't do alone, your "brother" and you may be able to accomplish together.

Remember the movie, "See no Evil, Hear no Evil" starring Richard Pryor and Gene Wilder. Richard was blind and Gene was deaf, but working together as a team, they were able to stay alive and overcome some deadly challenges.

I suggest to you, there are millions of old men and old women out there who have substantial assets, but who live alone, and who have few, if any, deserving heirs to whom to leave their estate. As already stated, 39 percent of women over 75 live alone.

Let's get creative. Get comfortable, pull up a chair, pour yourself a glass of your favorite beverage, and settle back. We are going to beat this old age conundrum to a pulp. (I was raised on a farm where a piece of haywire would fix anything; today, it's duct tape). Here we go, with an example of American ingenuity, and good old common sense.

Maggie Mae is a 79-year-old widow in failing health;

she lives alone in a large, modern house. She dreads the day she might be required to abandon her lovely home, and move into a nursing home. Maggie Mae has two children, a wayward son she has not seen in 25 years, and a daughter who is married to a rich doctor who lives in New Jersey. Honestly, Maggie Mae and her daughter are not that close.

Maggie Mae talked one time with her daughter about the day coming when she might not be able to live alone, and the daughter's only advice was to begin looking for an appropriate nursing home.

Along comes Rufus, a 74-year-old widower who is active and in decent health. Rufus lives from hand to mouth, with very few assets other than his car and personal effects. His only income is $1100 per month, and at times, he has financial difficulties.

Rufus and Maggie Mae meet in Piggly-Wiggly one day, and begin talking. She has a couple of small handy-man jobs that need to be done, and Rufus volunteers to come by and do the work for her. He's not charging her anything for his labor, but realistically, he is hoping for a tip.

As time passes, Rufus and Maggie Mae become trusted friends, with him spending more and more time helping her with little jobs around her house. She is becoming more and more dependent on Rufus' assistance.

One day, Maggie Mae reads an article about growing old, nursing homes, and Medicaid. She dreads moving into a nursing home, but what choice does she have? She decides to consult with an Elder Law attorney who tells her this:

a) If you move into a nursing home, you will only be

able to keep $2000 of that $106,000 you have in your savings account; the rest will go to pay your nursing home bill at the rate of $9,000 per month.

b) All of your $3500 per month retirement income will go to pay your nursing home bill, except $60 per month.

c) When the money runs out, Medicaid will start paying your bill, but Medicaid will file a lien against your home, and the lien must be paid at your death from the sale of the house. Two years of Medicaid reimbursement would completely consume the value of your house.

It occurs to Maggie Mae, not only might she lose everything, but she would lose it while a patient in a nursing home, the very place she does not want to be.

What if she hired someone to live in her home to help take care of her? All the money she would otherwise be paying to a nursing home, she can now spend on her personal care at home. She approaches Rufus with the idea of him moving into her guest room, and helping her out when she needs assistance.

"Oh, I can drive, go grocery shopping, clean the house, do the laundry; I cook a little bit, and I can take you to your doctor appointments, but I'm not much of a nurse," Rufus says.

"Rufus, with that kind of help from you, I can get by. I'm still able to do a lot for myself, and besides, I have the money to pay our living expenses, and I can afford visiting nurses and others to drop in as needed. You won't have to do anything you are uncomfortable doing."

So, they reached an agreement, and the arrangement worked well for both of them for four years. Eventually, Maggie Mae's health begins to deteriorate rapidly, and she and Rufus go again to consult with the Elder Law attorney.

"Maggie Mae, you still have $38,000 of your savings left, but if you go into a nursing home, you will lose $36,000 of that money, and you will lose almost all of your monthly retirement income. Remember, Medicaid will place a lien against your house to recover any money Medicaid pays on your nursing home bill. At $9,000 per month, the entire value of your home will be consumed in less than three years," said the lawyer.

"What can we do?" Maggie Mae asks. "At this point, I know I don't have much time left, and I'm more concerned about Rufus than I am myself. I want to help provide for Rufus; he's been a Godsend to me."

"Maggie Mae, you need to marry Rufus," her Elder Law attorney tells her.

"I love and respect Rufus, but I am not "in love" with him; I can't marry him!"

"If you marry Rufus, perhaps in name only, the $38,000 will be saved; that money will go into his pocket instead of the nursing home's pocket. Also, he will get the house free and clear if you want him to have it; there would be no Medicaid lien of any kind. Instead of Rufus having his $1100 retirement income, he will have that, plus about $2000 each month of your retirement income. Either he gets it, or the nursing home gets it."

"But if I do that, will I qualify for Medicaid to pay for my nursing home?"

"Yes, all that property is exempt if Rufus is your husband, and you will qualify for Medicaid, no problem. Also, by marrying Rufus and giving him all of this, he will be in a financial position to spend money on you while you are in the nursing home."

"What do you mean?" asked Maggie Mae.

"Rufus can pay the extra to get you the larger, private room, perhaps a nice TV, a motorized wheelchair, better clothes, more frequent visits by a hair stylist, a debit card so you can order online the little items that will bring you a little comfort and pleasure that the nursing home won't otherwise provide. Believe it or not, with a little outside help, the nursing home existence can be better . . . not great, but better."

So, they get married, and Maggie Mae moves into a nursing home three months later. Within a year, Maggie Mae dies after months of being semi-conscious. Rufus continues to live in the home which he now owns, and he enjoys a better standard of living than he has had in years.

Two years later, Rufus suffers a serious stroke, and suddenly he is not able to live his independent lifestyle. Prior to the stroke, Rufus had consulted with Maggie Mae's Elder Law attorney, and signed an Enhanced Power of Attorney, and an Advanced Medical Directive. His best friend, Ronnie, now serves as his trusted agent for all legal and medical issues.

Ronnie uses the $38,000 which is still in the bank, together with Rufus' $3100 monthly income to hire both medical caretakers and maintenance people to regularly go to Rufus' home to care for him. After a few months, Ronnie, as POA agent, sells the big house, and moves Rufus into a leased apartment which is handicap friendly, located in a senior community, and near Ronnie's home. Ronnie now has an additional $200,000 from the sale of the big house available to pay caretakers and others to keep Rufus comfortable in his own home.

Rufus is able to live at-home with excellent care for three more years when at the age of 81, he suffers a fatal stroke, leaving the remaining funds, $61,000 to his best buddy Ronnie.

Yes, the marriage was not for love; it was for convenience, but it was the cornerstone of a plan which allowed two elderly people to help each other have a much better quality of life in their final years.

There can be dozens of variations to the scheme described above. For one thing, all 50 states now recognize same-sex marriages, so the same arrangement could be accomplished between two men, or two women. Also, instead of marriage, contracts and irrevocable trust agreements can be constructed to accomplish the same objectives as demonstrated above, all without marriage or living together.

It does not have to be one senior and one caregiver; it could be an older senior couple who need help from a single caregiver, or a caregiver couple tending to one senior's needs.

If a strong relationship is established, there are many ways that property can be jointly titled where both the senior who needs services, and the caregiver who needs financial assistance, can mutually benefit. Jointly titled property pursuant to a caregiver contract won't violate Medicaid's eligibility rules, if properly done.

The goal to these plans is to avoid the nursing home

for as long as possible, maybe forever. In the hypothetical, Maggie Mae, a person of means, is probably headed to the nursing home without Rufus' help. Rufus who has no money, is certainly headed to a nursing home if he becomes unable to live independently without Maggie Mae's help. By helping each other, they both enjoy a high quality of life during all, or most, of their final years.

If you have no money, that's ok, but you have to bring something to the table. It can be as simple as providing pleasant companionship, or it may be more like a job where you render services. There are lots of opportunities out there, with more to come, but you can't wait until you are too old, too sick and no fun to be around.

As an Elder Law attorney, I see people who have followed in the footsteps of their parents, the Greatest Generation, by working hard, saving their money, and making smart investments. Those baby boomers are now arriving at old age with a pocketful of money and assets. Frequently, they have no heirs, or no deserving heirs, or their children are already financially secure.

I will be the first person to report anyone who is taking undue advantage of seniors; I am not suggesting that you act as a predator, but I am encouraging you to help seniors, and at the same time, help yourself.

Recently, I prepared a Will for a senior who is single with no children. She is leaving a multi-million-dollar estate to a person who has been her go-to person for the last ten years.

It pays to be nice, to be friendly, to be helpful.

Make a plan. Consult with an Elder Law Attorney. Be creative. Be bold!

One evening at the nursing home the attendant finds one of the guests rubbing shoe polish on his penis. The attendant asks why he is doing this.

He says, "They said it was daylight savings time."

The attendant says, "No no, sweetie. You're supposed to turn your clock back."

CHAPTER FOUR

Smoke and Mirrors

Believe it or not, there is still a little "playing room" for those of us who are, as they say, "financially-embarrassed". If you are too disagreeable to form a plan similar to the one Rufus made with Maggie Mae, or too lazy, or too proud, or if you simply prefer to fly solo, then you may be forced to seek financial assistance from the government.

There are many government programs floating around, some helpful, and some not so much, that are designed to aid indigent, sick or elderly citizens. It is beyond the scope of this guide to discuss all of these various programs. Our task is to develop plans for staying out of a nursing home, even though we might need skilled nursing care.

For better or for worse, Medicaid is the government's answer to citizens who are old, disabled, broke, and who cannot live without long term care. If we are looking for government assistance, then we are looking straight down Medicaid's barrel.

Medicaid is a federal program which is in place in all 50 states; however, each state has a certain amount of leeway as to the manner of implementing and regulating Medicaid within its borders. As a result, the amount and type of available care can vary greatly from one state to the next.

Every state has Medicaid programs which provide care benefits for persons residing outside the walls of a nursing home. Now, don't get too excited at this news, because as Homer (not Simpson) said, "there's many a slip 'twixt the cup and the lip."

The theory behind these programs is solid: many people who qualify for nursing home care can be cared for in a private home for less money than it takes to care for them in a nursing home. The government has implemented a variety of at-home programs on the premise that tax dollars can be saved. Good thinking! A rare phenomenon in legislative circles.

For example, if Joe has no money, and is unable to feed or dress himself, he is entitled to a nursing home bed which will cost the government approximately $8,000 or more each month. However, if the government agrees to pay Louie and his family $2,000 each month if they will take Joe in and take care of him, suddenly, Louie starts feeling a lot of brotherly love for old Joe.

The government spends another $1000 per month in visiting nurses and other services, to keep an eye on Joe while in Louie's home. The government still ends up saving thousands of dollars each month while meeting Joe's needs.

These programs seem to be a win-win-win; Joe is not institutionalized, Louie's family benefits financially, and the government saves a lot of money while taking care of its elderly. So, why haven't these programs dominated the field?

The answer to that question remains a mystery. These type of programs vary in detail from one state to the next, and often change annually, every time a state legislature meets. Fifty state legislatures meeting annually multiplies into a hodge-podge of ever-changing laws. It is far beyond the scope of this Guide to describe the debris carried downstream by this river of laws and regulations.

Suffice it to say, there are states who are very much in tune with the needs of their elderly, disabled populace, while other states seem to be casting a blind eye. In a report issued in 2020, sources reported that the state of New York spent over $12,000 per Medicaid recipient, while the state of New Mexico spent less than half that amount. The report ranks all the states, with Georgia coming in down towards the bottom at number 40, spending only a little over $5,000 per recipient.

While some of Georgia's programs look great on paper, they are not available to many needy citizens due to a lack of state funding. In fact, hundreds of people marched on Georgia's State Capitol in February of 2020 because of budget cuts to the state's Medicaid program. Over 7,000 people were on the waiting list when Georgia moved to cut the budget, not allowing any new recipients to be added.

Some approved applicants stated they had been on the State's waiting list for 4 years, 7 years, even 15 years, waiting for help they desperately needed, but which was not available due to limited funding.

While programs such as Georgia's "Medicaid Home- and Community-based Waiver Program" promise to help citizens avoid the nursing home route, the reality is quite different. Even the state brochure warns:

"Sometimes people may meet the criteria to receive Medicaid services . . . but may not receive services immediately. Funding for the programs is limited, and only a certain number of people can receive services based on available funds. This means there are nearly always people on waiting lists . . . ."

To further complicate things, where you stand in line is not necessarily determinative of who gets the next waiver. The State says:

"A person may be selected from the waiting list based on the severity of need, the availability of informal/family support, the length of time on the waiting list, and a person's continued eligibility for (paraphrased) nursing home care."

Sooooo, what's the importance of all this?

I remember as a personal injury attorney, before filing suit, I would investigate to determine what options I had as far as selecting the venue in which to file suit. South Georgia juries were notoriously stingy when awarding a Plaintiff damages for injuries he had received in a wreck. On the other hand, juries in metro Atlanta were much more generous.

A man could lose a leg in Moultrie, Georgia, and a local jury might give him $50,000 in damages, whereas, the same case might garner $500,000 from a Fulton County (Atlanta) jury.

The indigent person who seeks Medicaid benefits for home and community care might consider moving to a state which does a better job administering and funding such benefits. For example, if a man moved from Dyersburg, Tennessee, to Poplar Bluff, Missouri, a distance of 89.8 miles, he is now in Missouri which spends almost twice as much on each Medicaid recipient as Tennessee.

You can only apply for the benefits available in your state of residence, but you can change residence to another state on your own accord. Just make sure you follow the new state's protocol for establishing legal residency as early as possible, and prior to seeking benefits.

Admittedly, this is not a quick and easy fix, yet it is an option worth researching. Many of us have relatives or close friends scattered in several states; the possibility of moving to another state, possibly sharing space with friends or relatives, is worthy of consideration. **wallethub.com/edu/states-with-the-most-and-least-medicaid-coverage/71573**

Not long ago, I paid a social call on the attorney who gave me my first lawyer job. We talked about old times, and the practice of law. My friend who had been quite successful, hinted at one reason for his success:

"Keith, I always tried to stay where the money was!"

I smiled, remembering that he always managed to stay in the same lane with the movers and shakers in our hometown.

Better days ahead?

If we know the problem, and we know the solution, and the laws are already on the books, then why are we in such a mess? Every high school football coach knows the answer to that question: execution, execution, execution.

Recent events may cause our lawmakers who control funding, and the bureaucrats who regulate the industry, to tighten up. The Covid-19 pandemic might serve as a big wake-up call on many levels. Nursing homes and other long-term care facilities were virtual death traps for their residents when the virus came visiting. While the fatality numbers vary substantially, there is no doubt a large percentage of those who died from the virus were institutionalized, elderly patients.

For example, in my home state of Georgia which fared better than some places, and worse than others, approximately 20 percent of all Covid-related deaths were nursing home patients. Thousands of elderly residents died, despite living in a **skilled-nursing** environment!

The lesson to be learned is that nursing homes are easy targets for any virus or other contagious disease. Can you imagine if some of the more contagious strains of Covid had struck before vaccines were developed? One recent report indicates one of the mutant strains is 45 percent more contagious than Covid-19.

One thing is for certain, pandemics do exist; they are real. When will the next one occurr? How contagious will it be? How deadly will it be? How long before we can bring it under control? Who wants to be in a nursing home when it hits?

It is anticipated that state legislatures will begin doing a better job of designing and funding nursing home alternatives; do your research and see which states are doing the best job. You may love Tennessee, but you might prefer living in an apartment in Missouri with the state's help, rather than living in a shared Medicaid room in Memphis.

Rumor has it that New York state has excellent at-home Medicaid benefits.

Regardless, as previously stated, exhaust all other possible remedies before settling on a plan which may be blown about by the whimsy of political winds.

What do you tell your grandmother when she doesn't want to go to a nursing home?

"It won't be for long."

CHAPTER FIVE

Let's all dance.

In the preceding chapters, I focused on the wealthy and the poor, and made suggestions as to how those two groups should, or possibly could, avoid a nursing home finale. In this chapter, I will focus on the rest of us.

Most of us, unfortunately, don't have an old age plan; we just keep living on a hope and a prayer that everything will turn out all right. One researcher suggested many people simply cannot visualize being unable to feed themselves, or unable to toilet without assistance, or helpless to do any of the other ADL's. Since a person cannot see himself being in such a predicament, he may be reluctant to make a plan.

That is exactly why I have written this Guide, to educate and to motivate the reader, and to facilitate the plan-making process. The primary goal for now, for the future, and forever more, is to stay out of the nursing home.

To those people who refuse to forge any kind of a plan . . . good luck! My only question is, why are you still reading this?

Ok, I'll make one last effort. You buy car insurance, house insurance, trip insurance. You don't plan to have a wreck, or to burn your house down, or to cancel that long-awaited vacation, but you still take precautionary measures.

The worst thing that can happen when you have an old age plan, is that you don't get to use it, i.e., you never need long term care. That's like complaining, I've carried car insurance for all of these years, and never had a wreck. What a blessing, if that were to happen.

But if you do live long enough to need long term care, and you don't have a plan, then, the chances are you will either self-pay, perhaps until all of your lifetime savings are gone, or, you will end up in a nursing home, or both!

As an Elder Law attorney, I have studied ad nauseum all the laws, rules, and regulations as to how a person can preserve his assets, and still be qualified to receive Medicaid benefits. What benefits, you may ask? Why, payment of nursing home bills, naturally, which are the only benefits you can count on being available. The at-home waiver benefits are famous for not being available for thousands of people who are qualified to receive them . . . lack of funding, remember?

The thrust of this Guide is **not** to save all of your assets in an effort to secure for you a free Medicaid bed in a nursing home, but rather to keep you out of the nursing home, period.

The first fork in the road is a big deal. You must decide what is most important to you: spending your money to stay out of a nursing home, spending your money on something else, or leaving lots of money to your children when you die.

As judges say, this decision presents a question of first impression; neither the rich nor the poor, whom we have covered in prior chapters, usually get caught up in this dilemma. The rich have plenty of money to go around, and the poor have no money either to save, to spend, or to leave to their heirs.

If you choose to blow your money on fun things, like boats, beach houses, and European vacations, I say go for it! Party down and have fun. No criticism from me whatsoever. You may never need long term care, anyway, so what's all the fuss? And if you live to be old and need long term care, look over at the guy in the bed beside you, chances are it's me! Your nursing home roommate!

On the other hand, if you prefer to save your assets for family members, then I have two pieces of advice: first, call early tomorrow morning and make an appointment with an Elder Law attorney, one with a good reputation. The last thing you want is to end up in a nursing home and all of your assets be confiscated by Medicaid, otherwise known as the "worst case scenario".

No, you should not wing it based on your cousin Elmo's advice to put everything into a corporation, or to add your son's name to the CDs, or to set up a revocable trust.

The second piece of advice is to start researching nursing homes. All nursing homes are not created equal; some are better than others. Your goal is to locate one which is the least-rotten of the lot. Good luck.

And then, there's all the other folks, the nervous nellies who do want a plan, and who are ready to get started.

A common situation is where Polly, a single lady, 74 years old, who has an income of $2000, a savings of $80,000, and a home worth $140,000. An elder law attorney can assist her, and with a little preplanning, possibly save all of those assets and still get Polly qualified immediately for Medicaid coverage to pay the $9000 per month nursing home bill.

Is that what she really wants to do?

Another option, is to utilize all those resources to buy in-home care for as long as possible. For example, if she sells the house, she can add $140,000 to the $80,000 to establish a war chest of $220,000, plus her monthly income.

The obvious question is, how long will she be able to stay at home?

If Polly's living expenses, including apartment rent, and in-home services by medical professionals and caretakers is $7,000 per month. Then the burn rate against her war chest is $5,000 per month (7,000 minus monthly income of 2000). At that rate, it would take 3 years and 8 months before her money is gone.

A 2018 study revealed that on average, women needed 2.5 years of long-term care as compared to men who needed only 1.5 years of long-term care. Only 14 percent of all women would need 5 years or more of long-term care. Yes, the numbers about "how long" a person will need care are all over the board, not to mention that every case is different.

In this example, the odds are Polly will be able to self-pay for in-home care for as long as she will need it. If she is still alive when her money runs out, she will immediately qualify for Medicaid, and continue to receive care in the dreaded nursing home.

Every case is different, but Polly's example demonstrates the basics of a simple plan. The beauty of this plan is she or her agent can decide which caregivers and medical professionals come into her home, how often they come, and she never has to get pre-approved, or file proof of claims, or beg for reimbursement of expenses. She and her money are in control, and if she wants to hire a daughter, granddaughter, or friend to perform various services, she has the discretion to do so.

Granted, three years and eight months is not a long time generally speaking, but for an elderly person with serious health issues, it could possibly be long enough. Additionally, Polly might also be able to receive some Medicare and Medicaid benefits to supplement her out-of-pocket expenses, and be able to extend the time even further.

While every case is different, there are some common factors in every situation which need to be considered as a person contemplates his own situation:

a. *The needs of the patient.* Is the patient only unable to bathe and dress (two of the ADL's) without assistance? While this condition would medically qualify him for a bed in a skilled-care nursing home, it is quite possible to meet those needs in-home with caregivers.

b. *Costs to cover those needs.* On the other hand, a patient who needs help with all six of the ADL's would require a lot more attention, and at a much greater cost, perhaps approaching or even exceeding the magic number of $9,000 per month for round-the-clock, 7-day-a-week care.

c. *Patient preferences.* The plan should obviously

consider those options which are preferred by the patient. Does the patient prefer living alone, or perhaps with a live-in caretaker, or even in a group care home. A person who relishes privacy, and who does not play well with others, probably would not be happy in a group home. On the other hand, a social butterfly who has physical limitations, but a sharp wit, may blossom in a shared-home setting.

d. *Availability of options.* A person who wants to stay near his hometown of Meigs, Georgia, a rural, bucolic setting, may not have the same options as a person who prefers living in cosmopolitan, upscale Buckhead, a suburb of Atlanta, Georgia.

As noted, the greater the dependency, the more money it will take to meet the needs. The more money spent, the sooner funds will be exhausted, leaving perhaps no choice, but a Medicaid bed in a nursing home.

A resource that is sometimes overlooked is the cash surrender value of a life insurance policy, or the cash-out of an annuity. A reverse mortgage can provide cash against real estate that is currently unmarketable for some reason. This is not the time to wear your "investor" cap; we are in survival, quality of life mode.

A patient may have family or friends who would be happy to contribute either their time or money to help care for a loved one or a dear friend. Often, the only prerequisite is for the patient to reach out and ask for help or to relate the need.

I am constantly amazed at the outpouring of love

and money that Americans are willing to contribute, once they recognize a need. It happens over and over again, many times between rank strangers. Don't be too proud to ask for help; you will be surprised at the number and caliber of people who will respond favorably.

Over time, quality of life can, and usually does, deteriorate, even when a person is being cared for in his own home by loving attendants and dedicated medical providers. When the reasoning behind keeping a person at home no longer bears fruit due to the patient's mental and/or physical state, then it may be time to place the person in a nursing home. A person who is totally bedridden, who sleeps most of the time, and who appears to have no cognitive abilities remaining, might not suffer any detriment to be confined in a nursing home. Transferring the now mostly-empty vessel to the nursing home will relieve some of the burden, emotional and otherwise, being carried by the loved ones.

In the next section, end-of-life choices will be addressed. Whether the person is receiving care at home, or in a nursing home, or somewhere else, he has the right to know, and to be free to act upon, the choices he has when the end of life approaches. As the right to death movement grows, a person will have the opportunity to die on terms very much different from the slow, grueling process that is often the norm in many states today.

There are two old men at a nursing home. One of them turns to the other and asks "Do you wear boxers or briefs?

"The other man responds "Depends"

CHAPTER SIX

Staying out of the Nursing home with Care Insurance

Elder Law attorneys are trained to develop plans whereby a person can have his cake and eat it, too; in other words, arrange a person's assets so he can retain ownership in one form or the other, and still qualify for Medicaid to pay his nursing home bill. The problem is, a plan to qualify for Medicaid is usually a plan to spend your last days in a nursing home. Currently, you cannot depend on Medicaid to pay for long term care in your home. This may not be true in all states, but it is certainly true in Georgia and many other states.

If Medicaid is not going to pay for your in-home care, who is?

That leaves only two suspects, self-pay and insurance. We have already examined the self-pay possibilities, now it's time to look at insurance.

Some readers may think Medicare pays for long term care, but as a general rule, it does not. Medicare will pay limited benefits, but those are usually associated with a person getting well, or improving, perhaps rehab care. Helping a person with their ADL's, long term, is not Medicare's job.

Long term care policies have tumbled in popularity over the last 20 years, from over 750,000 insureds in 2002 to 56,000 in 2018, a drop of 92 percent; many of the carriers have simply dropped out of the market. This fall from grace may be connected in part to the low public appeal nursing homes have; nursing homes and traditional long term care policies have historically gone hand in hand.

For the last several years, the insurance industry has been struggling to find an insurance product which would win public approval. Now that the pandemic has hit with so many nursing home deaths, the call to arms . . . finding an alternative to nursing homes as well as a corresponding care policy . . . is at a fever pitch.

When I began my research, I was searching for policies which paid benefits solely for at-home care; I was not interested in policies that contained nursing home benefits.

Initially, I found policies which provided greater at-home benefits than in the past, yet, those policies were still loaded with benefits for patients residing in nursing homes.

As I continued to look, I began to discover insurance products which are relatively new on the market. One of the first I found was a plan underwritten by Aetna called the Home Care Plus plan. A person can choose a plan that will pay up to $1200 per week payable directly to the patient for up to 52 weeks to cover medical services rendered in the patient's home. The trigger is that the services must be medically necessary, and must include a minimum of three practitioner visits of one hour each per week.

This Aetna policy seems to be more user-friendly than traditional long-term care policies. For example, the underwriting requirements are much less stringent, allowing a person to apply and get an answer in a short period of time. Aetna even accepts applications for clients up to 89 years of age. The money is paid directly to the insured without the hassle of precertification, and the client can choose a no-waiting elimination option. The policy is guaranteed renewable, and there are several ways to pay the premium.

If a client has selected the $1200 a week option, and receives three medical visits in one week costing a total of $800, the client still gets the $1200, $400 above actual costs.

As with most insurance policies, there are a number of riders which can be added, such as a cancer rider paying a lump sum amount if the client is diagnosed with cancer. Emergency room visits and ambulance trips can also be covered by adding the appropriate rider.

This Aetna policy is an example of what the industry is calling a "short-term care" or "anti-nursing home" policy; it is sometimes referred to as a "recovery care" policy.

Other companies are rolling out policies similar to the Aetna policy; for example, Medico, an AARP sponsored short term policy, recently gave me a quote of $398. per month for coverage for a 73-year-old man who wanted 360 days of benefits, at $300 per day, with 0 days waiting period. For a total cost of $4776., I would be able to buy potential coverage of $108,000. This was for the top level of coverage offered.

The American Association for Long-Term Care Insurance found the more typical premium for a 65-year-old would be $105 per month, and for a 70-year-old, $141. A collateral benefit is that the policy pays in addition to any Medicare payments for the same expenses, while long-term care insurance typically does not pay if Medicare pays.

Traditional long term care policies have simply been too expensive for a lot of American pocketbooks; however, with the short-term policies, come much-reduced premiums. The theory is, to have some care coverage is better than none at all. The companies are quick to point out that according to the short-term care advisory center, 49 percent of long-term care claims last less than one year. If that holds true, a short-term policy is all the coverage needed in a large number of cases. www.insurance.com/health/short-term-care.html

I return to my point, do your research to get the best result. There is a wealth of information online which will allow you to find the policy that best fits your situation. For example the website mentioned in the preceding paragraph has an article entitled, "Is short-term care coverage right for you?"

A word of caution: a lot of the articles online are written by agents who are promoting the insurance products they sell . . . their report may not be completely objective. Also, there are other companies which post opinions and op-eds while promoting their services as financial advisors or managers. Most of these posts are informative and well-worth reading, just be aware of any "ulterior" motives.

There is an organization, the National Association of Insurance Commissioners, "NAIC" which supposedly provides the public with unbiased information. NAIC has a publication entitled, "A Shopper's Guide to Long-Term Care Insurance" which is 71 pages of pertinent information. Some states require an insurance company to give a copy of this booklet to any prospect before signing him up for insurance (Georgia does not). For a downloadable copy of this booklet, go to www.naic.org/documents/ prod_serv_consumer_ltc_lp.pdf

More tips about care insurance

There are still carriers selling long term policies, and policies have been rewritten over the last few years in response to what the public wants... flexibility and options. It is my prediction the public will begin to turn more and more to obtaining insurance, whether long term, short term, hybrid or other.

A care insurance policy is similar to any other insurance policy; the basic concept is to spread the risk. If 50 people buy fire insurance to cover their house, the odds are that not more than one house in the 50 will be destroyed by fire. The 50 premiums coming in gives the insurance company enough money to reimburse the poor fellow who loses his house, with a nice bit of change left over for the insurance company.

While 49 people paid premiums and never received any financial return, the fellow who lost his house paid only $5,000 in premiums for the $200,000 dollar insurance check he received when his house burned.

Who to talk to first?

Sometimes a person buys a policy from an insurance

agent who is an old family friend, or perhaps a fellow church member, or maybe from the daughter of a friend. But remember, this is not a social affair, but a complicated business deal where lots of big decisions are being made which involve lots of money … big premiums to be paid in, and perhaps big benefits to be paid out.

Sitting down cold with an insurance agent, no matter who he is, is not the best place to begin. While the agent may know the policy he is attempting to sell, he may not know your priorities, your financial situation, your estate plan, and all the other things which make up the BIG picture.

I suggest you sit down with an Elder Law attorney or a professional financial manager, and do some preliminary work to determine:

a)   Do you need Care Insurance; and
b)   What type of policy best fits with your overall plan.

When you go car shopping, do you put some time and thought into the process before you arrive at the dealership? Of course, you do. Buying care insurance is a lot more complicated, and can be a lot more expensive.

Who can afford to buy Care Insurance?

The first time Long-Term Care Insurance is mentioned, the client will normally respond, "But isn't that awfully expensive?"

The correct answer is, "Anything related to health care is expensive."

The real question is, "Can I afford it?" As a general rule of thumb, if the premium charged for your policy is not more than 7 percent of your income, then the purchase of insurance is recommended. Also, if you are able to pay the premiums without affecting your lifestyle, or negatively impacting your savings or overall net worth, then by all means, buy the insurance.

When to get the Insurance

With the advent of short-term or anti-nursing home policies, the ability to get coverage has gotten a lot easier; the underwriting requirements are much easier to pass. Most short-term carriers offer policies to applicants in their 80's! With long term care, the story is entirely different.

When you apply for long term care insurance, you will be closely scrutinized to see whether you meet underwriting requirements . . .to see if you are healthy enough for the company to insure your care. The company is looking for healthy, young applicants. Unfortunately, the rejection rate is approximately 45 percent, and this is largely a group of people who applied, thinking they would be healthy enough to pass. People with known health problems usually don't even apply.

There is a balance to be struck between applying too early, and waiting too late. If you apply when you are 50 and healthy, you may pay a long time before ever making a claim, however your premiums are significantly cheaper.

If you wait until you are 65, you have presumably saved money, yet you have run the risk of experiencing a health event which would terminate your eligibility for coverage, and of course, your premiums are significantly higher. The premium structure is said to be weighted, so in most cases, waiting to get coverage does not save money in the long run.

The experts say obtaining insurance between the age of 60 and 65 is the optimum time in most cases. Your personal medical history, or family genes, can influence your "starting date". For example, if Alzheimer's, dementia, or other progressively disabling diseases run in your family, you might consider buying insurance earlier. On the other hand, if you come from a blessed bloodline which enjoys good health long into their lives, you might want to wait until you are in your late 60's, or even early 70's.

Listed below are some policy features which you should thoroughly investigate before writing that check for your first premium:

1. Is the policy "tax-qualified", meaning you can deduct off your income taxes the premiums you pay, and any benefits paid to you are not taxable income.

Normally, you cannot deduct premiums for hybrid policies which are life insurance policies with long-term care riders attached. Check with your accountant.

2. Is the policy qualified for "state partnership"? Certain policies are favored by the states, and if you buy one of these policies, you are entitled to certain benefits, like keeping more of your assets if you must ever apply for Medicaid benefits. Again, hybrid policies with life insurance are generally not partnership policies.

3. If you are a couple, do you really need to insure both spouses? While couple discounts are normally given, and benefits may be shareable between spouses, an older spouse may cause pre-

miums to be much higher.

Many times, the sole surviving spouse, who is usually the younger wife, is the one who will need protection the most in her old age. Getting a policy just for the younger, healthier spouse, will result in a big savings on the amount of premium to be paid.

4. Is the policy guaranteed renewable? Is the premium fixed, or will it be going up as time passes? If you become sick or disabled and begin receiving benefits, are future premiums waived? Does the policy ever become a "paid up policy"? For example, no claims in 10 years, no more premiums?

Or, must you pay premiums forever?

5. Does the policy offer an inflation rider? For younger insureds, this is a very important provision, because it may be years before a claim is made. Experts often recommend a 3 to 5 percent, compounded, inflation rider.

6. The elimination period (waiting period or deductible) is very important. If it is a 90-day elimination period, does this mean 90 calendar days (consecutive days starting the first day an insured is entitled to benefits) or do benefits start only after RECEIVING care for 90 days? In other words, if you receive care three days per week, is the entire week (7 days) counted against the elimination period, or is only the 3 days you actually received care counted towards satisfying the waiting period?

7. Is the maximum benefit calculated based on

maximum daily benefit, or maximum monthly benefit? For at-home care, this is very important, because the same service is not rendered every day. If you are planning to stay at home, ALWAYS choose to have the maximum benefit computed as maximum monthly benefit.

8. Are benefits paid on a "reimbursable" basis, or "indemnity" basis? If it is reimbursable, you must submit claim forms proving the expense you paid before it is reimbursed to you. Indemnity means the cash is paid directly to you, and you make the disbursement to providers.

9. Are you entitled to choose your caregivers? Can you hire family members or others who live with you? Does the insurance company have the right to approve the caregivers in advance?

10. Does the policy provide you with a free care manager: a person who coordinates the care you are to receive, and who establishes a plan of care within policy guidelines? This can be very important for the senior who does not have others assisting her in arranging provider services.

11. Does the policy provide a "cash surrender value"? If you ever apply for Medicaid, you will be required to cash in the policy, and the cash value will then be counted against you as far as your financial eligibility for Medicaid benefits.

12. If you pay a large lump sum premium (sometimes charged on hybrid policies), is this payment considered to be a prohibited transfer of assets if done within 5 years of applying for Me-

dicaid?

13. Be careful not to over-insure, i.e., buying too much coverage. A two-year, $200 per day benefit will normally satisfy the requirement for the policy to be considered a "state partnership" policy.

Many unbiased experts agree that anything more than a 3-year term is probably excessive, based on statistics. Of course, the longer the term, the larger the premium. Picking the right term for you might cause the premium to fall within your budget.

14. The experts recommend that the insurance carrier you go with, be ranked in the top two categories by A.M. Best, Dun and Bradstreet, or other rating companies. Make the agent show you the carrier's rating.

15. Read the online reviews, check the Better Business Bureau ratings, ask the agent to give you names of others in the community who have had experience filing claims on the same policies.

A word about so-called "hybrid policies". My research indicates these policies are first and foremost, insurance policies, with long term care a lesser consideration. They are very appealing, if you can afford the big up-front premiums, because you or your heirs eventually get your money back. Because they do not qualify for tax deductions on the premiums, do not qualify as "partnership" policies, are not very "Medicaid-compliant," and do not provide the best long-term care features, they need to be very closely scrutinized.

At the very least, when considering a hybrid policy, compare it with the alternative: a separate life insurance policy combined with a separate care policy. For the same money, maybe a little less, or maybe a little more, you might get a good life insurance policy, and a much better care policy.

Lastly, I have discovered a company, American Senior Services, Inc, which offers a service contract for in-home assistance with the ADL's (remember, the activities of daily living). Technically, this is not insurance, but a plan where you pay a fee and enter into a contract. The company then provides non-medical people to come into your home to help with cooking, cleaning, toileting, dressing, accompanying you to your appointments, and other things many seniors need assistance with. The fee you pay corresponds with the number of hours of service you are entitled to receive.

I like this idea, because there is no underwriting, no waiting period, no age limit, very little paperwork, and the services can be performed by your friends or other people you choose . . . except no live-in's or family members can be paid. The services can be 24/7, 7 days per week.

A short-term care policy, such as Aetna's, providing medical services inside the home, and a separate contract to provide non-medical services, may be the best plan yet for comprehensive at-home care.

I am digging deeper into this service contract idea which is known as "True Freedom:" in fact, I spoke by telephone yesterday with the CEO of the company and will continue to communicate with them to learn more.

I plan to have information and various materials available at my office concerning that company and the different contracts they offer. Further, I am considering being a producer for that company, so beware! **truefreedomhomecare.com**

My basic suggestions (your family health history might alter these):

> **Put your dollars into policies which provide at-home care.**

> **If you are 70 years of age or more, look into the anti-nursing home policies, and see if your budget will allow you to buy coverage of at least $600 per week.**

> **If you are between 60 and 70, stick with the long-term care policies if you can afford one, buying at least $6000 per month coverage for at least two years with a 3 percent compounded inflation rider, and a zero-waiting period.**

> **Reread the 15 features discussed above, and fit as many of those favorable features as possible into your policy.**

> **If you have money that is not working for you, invest in some coverage and put that money to work.**

> **Scrutinize the hybrid policies; compare them with separate life insurance and care policies before buying.**

This drunk wanders into a hotel lounge where an insurance convention just happens to be taking place. The drunk is hell-bent on causing trouble and he yells, "I think all insurance agents are crooks, and if anyone doesn't like it, come up and do something about it."

Straight away, this guy runs up to him and says angrily, "Hey! You take that back right now!"

The drunk sneers and asks, "Why, are you an agent?"

The man replies, "No, I'm a crook."

IN CONCLUSION

America is about to face a dire situation as the senior care crisis comes closer. As with any approaching object, the nearer it comes, the larger it looms. Whether our governments, federal and states', will be able to properly manage the flood of elderly, ailing seniors that will roll across our Nation over the next few decades, is anyone's guess.

The primary purpose of this Guide is to serve as a call for individual action. Every thinking, mature person needs to be working on his own plan; no one is helpless or without remedy. The goal is to secure a higher quality of life during one's last days, and the working assumption, is to age somewhere, anywhere, other than in a public, nursing home.

The financially-successful retiree has the means for devising a grand plan for his care during his failing-health years; but will he take the initiative and do it?

The financially-insecure must find another way to skin the cat. He cannot afford to hire someone to build his castle, but with a little effort, a little American ingenuity, a little boldness, he is perfectly capable of building his own. The materials he needs are lying around everywhere; it's just a matter of getting started.

There will be some governmental assistance for those who strive to age at-home, but seeking those benefits will look more like an Easter Egg hunt than a soup line. Any chance of success will depend upon how informed the senior stays, how creative, and how flexible he is willing to be, to capture the prize. Do not expect at-home government care benefits to find you in the crowd.

For the average American who has lived the dream, at least partially, the complexity of the task ahead is daunting, but that is no reason to be stilled. I can give no better advice than the favorite expression of an old friend of mine: "Start where you are, with what you have, and do the best you can."

Make a plan to utilize your resources towards achieving the goals you have set. You may not be able to devise and implement a fail-safe plan; there may be risks, assumptions, and uncontrolled factors at play. Regardless, your chances of success are greatly enhanced if you jump off the track as the speeding train approaches.

Make a plan, Stan!

SECTION TWO

End Life Options

CHAPTER SEVEN

Elvis has left the Building.
Maybe not.

What's all this junk about end-of-life options?

I thought the rules were simple and well-understood:

*You live as long as you possibly can.

*Doctors will do everything they can to keep you alive as long as possible.

Case closed.

That may have been the societal norm in the past, but I doubt even the most-devout Catholic in Boston would agree with those ideas in 2021. You would probably get thrown out of Sloppy Joe's in Key West for espousing such primitive views. Heaven forbid, you start a thread advocating those ideas on social media!

Everyone is aware that medical science has developed the equipment and the know-how to keep the heart beating when it wants to stop, to force oxygen through the body even though lungs have collapsed, and to bypass your stomach, intestines, and other organs to feed nutrients, antibiotics, hormones, and whatever else your body might need, directly into your mechanically-pumped bloodstream.

The historical road to death was fairly straight, short and narrow, but now, with the advances of medical science, there are lots of detours, loops, bypasses, and alternate routes making the trip much more complicated, and sometimes much longer.

Because of all of this intermeddling, situations arise sometimes where a person's body can land somewhere between life and death. To explain this, the experts decided there were actually two stages to the process of dying: "clinical death" and "biological death."

Clinical death happens first, and is usually defined as when your heart stops beating and your lungs stop pumping oxygen. At this point, you are clinically dead, and you won't be coming back unless something is done, perhaps divine intervention, to get both systems up and running again. An example of clinical death is when a person goes into cardiac arrest. The heart stops beating and within seconds, you stop breathing and fall unconscious.

The good news is that you may not be gone yet. You can be brought back from clinical death, if CPR and other methods are used to restart the heart, usually within four minutes. If the heart begins beating again, the lungs go back to work, and you are alive! Just as alive, albeit standing on a banana peel, as you ever were.

Once someone has stopped breathing, he has about 4-6 minutes until brain damage begins to occur. At around 6-10 minutes, some brain damage is likely to be taking place. Generally speaking, after 10 minutes, irreversible brain damage has almost certainly occurred. Within a few more minutes, the brain is so damaged, it stops functioning- no electrical activity, and at this point you are not only brain dead and biologically dead, you are never-coming-back dead.

Over the last one-hundred years, medical science has developed the knowledge necessary to prevent a vital system from shutting down. A person may be on the path to certain death, but along comes kidney dialysis, radiation, open-heart surgery, and a host of other procedures, which not only delay, but in many cases, prevents death from occurring.

John Prestwich at age 17 became paralyzed from the chin down, unable to breathe on his own. For the next 16 years, he was in an iron lung in a hospital. He lived a total of 50 years, only 5 minutes away from death if his respirator failed. Similarly, Patricia LeBlack, was kept alive for 40 years due to continuous kidney dialysis.

Experts generally agree, bodily functions can be maintained indefinitely by artificial means. Remove the machines, the body suffers clinical death, and without intervention, biological death.

If a person is brain dead, he is biologically dead; he is DEAD-DEAD! The fact that machines can keep his heart beating and his lungs working, does not mean he is alive. He is still dead, even though parts of his body are functioning the same way they did when he was alive.

Death can also be cheated when an old defunct heart is removed, and replaced with a healthy donor heart. There have been approximately 25,000 heart transplants in the US over the last 45 years with the longest survivor, according to one source, living 33 years with a donor heart before dying.

Along with all these medical miracles come questions; ethical and legal questions about who decides which patient gets all of this extended care. For example, who decides which patient gets a donor heart?

It is estimated that 50,000 people around the world are waiting on heart transplant lists, yet only 5000 can expect a new heart; the other 45,000 will likely die from their heart problems. The difference between life and death in some of those cases amount to little more than the luck of the draw.

With heart transplants, there exists The American Society of Transplantation which publishes "recommendations" as to which patients should be considered for transplantation. Another organization, The United Network for Organ Sharing, has created a "system" to ensure donor hearts are distributed fairly. Some of the criteria are: time on the wait list, severity of illness, and geographic distance between the donor hospital and the transplant center.

In other cases, it may be a pharmaceutical company that decides if a person gets a life-saving drug simply by pricing the miracle cure beyond the financial reach of many people. Or, an insurance company may be the decision-maker by classifying a drug as "experimental", and therefore not covered by the policy.

The question posed by William Shakespeare, "To be, or not to be . . ." is now often answered by someone or some entity other than the person whose ox is in the ditch.

Remember the case of Terri Schiavo, a young woman whose brain was severely damaged, but not dead . . . there was some brain activity. She was kept alive on life support for 15 years while her husband and her parents fought in state and federal courts over whether the husband had the right to remove Terri from life support. She was not biologically-dead, since there was some brain activity, but her diagnosis was "a persistent and irreversible vegetative state". Eventually the plug was pulled, and she suffered clinical and biological death approximately two weeks later.

Consider the case of an 86-year-old man who has lived for years in a nursing home due to advanced Alzheimer's. He suddenly experiences cardiac arrest. Who makes the decision whether or not to restart his engine?

For many of us, we will never have an option. We will suffer a heart attack while alone on the back 40 acres, and be dead as a doornail when someone finds us. Others will have their bodies mangled in car wrecks, and neither medical science nor all of Humpty Dumpty's men can put the person back together again. Too many will be intentionally killed by a murderer, or accidentally grab a highly-charged electrical wire, or ... and the list is endless.

There was a television series that ran for several years entitled, "1000 Ways to Die" playing reenactments of many of the strange and bizarre ways people have died.

In many other cases, there is a moment in time, when someone has to make a decision, do we continue to provide medical care to keep this person alive, or do we stop, and let him die.

About 50 years ago, someone had the novel idea to let the PATIENT decide! Of course, this meant the patient must decide IN ADVANCE as to the medical treatment he would prefer to receive in certain situations. As a result of such forward thinking, the "Living Will" was born; a document to be signed by an individual describing his preferences for care in certain situations. Louis Kutner, an Indiana attorney, is the person credited with drawing the first Living Will in 1967.

Thirty years ago, I was in my office meeting with an elderly gentleman who wanted me to prepare a Will for him. During the conversation, I asked him if he wanted a "living Will", and I explained a living Will was a document in which he could decide if he wanted to be hooked up to machines to be kept alive.

The fellow, who was clearly old-school, with little formal education, looked at me, and said:

"No, Mr. Murphy. I won't be needing that paper. When the Old Master calls me home, ain't no machine gonna keep me alive!"

I didn't disagree with him.

This Guide is going to take a look at the role the patient has, or should have, in deciding the care he should be given during the final stages of life. When should medical science stop helping the patient live, and when, if at all, should medical science help the patient die?

An old man was on his death bed and had less than a day to live. As he lay there reflecting on his life, he smelled his favorite cookies in the kitchen.

So using his last bit of will and effort, he dragged himself out of bed and crawled to the kitchen for a cookie.

He sat down at the table and reached for one when his wife popped his hand with a wooden spoon: "Don't touch it! Those are for your funeral!"

CHAPTER EIGHT

"I know my Rights . . . ."

My grandmother on my daddy's side had some ailment eighty years ago which caused her a tremendous amount of pain. An old doctor prescribed narcotics to dull the pain, and unfortunately, my grandmother became addicted to opiates; her life slowly went downhill.

I will never forget as a young boy, sitting at the supper table that night many years ago, when Granddaddy came in and said to my father, "Son, your Mama is gone!"

Daddy immediately jumped up from the table, and Granddaddy explained that Grandmother was missing, and a search party was being assembled to look for her.

A few hours later, some neighbors found a long, black cloak floating in a nearby pond; my grandmother's body was soon recovered. Grandmother had committed suicide, slipping out of the house when darkness fell, dressed in black clothes, and then a quick trip to a nearby pond. It was obvious she had planned her death.

I remember a man, a few years back, who was a regular in our trail-riding club. He was a jovial fellow, always in a good mood, and a lot of fun to be around. He had a gravelly voice due to throat cancer which he had survived several years before. A friend called me one day and told me the man had committed suicide; I was shocked to hear of his death, especially by his own hand.

A relative explained the man had stayed around the house that morning, doing one honey-do job after the other for his wife. Eventually, he asked her, "Doll, is there anything else I can do for you?" She replied, "No, you've done enough."

The man then took his pistol, went into the back yard, and put a .38 bullet into his head. I later learned his throat cancer had come back, and his doctor had told him it was just a matter of time. My friend chose to die on his own terms.

Another sad experience of this type hit even closer to home. There was a friend of mine who dropped by my law office one day and asked me if he could make a change to his Will. As we talked, I realized he wanted me to drop what I was doing, and change his Will immediately. I began to worry, so I questioned him for some time, and he eventually confessed that he was contemplating suicide.

I cancelled the remaining appointments I had that afternoon, and spent the next three hours talking to my friend. I refused to change his Will, anything to make him slow down and come to his senses. During our talk, his mood changed, and by the time he left my office, I thought he was out of danger.

I was shocked when I heard two days later, he had driven down to his favorite place on Earth, the beach at Daytona, and had shot himself in the head around sun up. Almost every time I see a pretty sunrise, especially coming up over the ocean, I think of my friend whom I was unable to save.

In the three cases I have cited, all of the individuals were well known to me. They were all good, law-abiding people; however, questions arise any time a person takes his own life. Discussing end-of-life options might also give rise to some of the same questions.

In my opinion, promoting this Guide is not much different from peddling fresh fish. The options presented here, just like fish, need to pass the smell test before being offered up.

It's difficult to find the correct word with which to label this discussion.

"Suicide" is defined as "the intentional taking of one's life."

"Euthanasia" is defined as "the painless killing of a patient who suffers from an incurable and painful disease."

Neither of these terms, standing alone, accurately capture the concept which this Guide is focused on.

The term "suicide" embraces a lot of circumstances which don't fit into the context of our conversation. It could mean a person who chooses to end his life because he is facing financial disaster; I remember stories of people jumping out of tall buildings on Wall Street when the stock market crashed at the beginning of the Great Depression. Or suicide may accurately describe a broken-hearted lover pulling the trigger on himself when he discovers his true love has betrayed him. Another example, a criminal killing himself to escape justice; the list of motives for taking one's own life is almost endless.

"Euthanasia" seems to involve another person who makes the decision to end another's life in order to end his pain and suffering. It is often used in the context of a person putting his pet to sleep when the pet is faced with an incurable and painful disease or injury. Pet euthanasia is widely embraced; it is considered to be an act of love and compassion.

It is very easy to get caught up in a semantic debate, a war of words between people who hold opposing viewpoints. To do so, reminds me of a hypothetical one of my professors used in law school in a criminal justice class:

"A woman intentionally pushes her husband out of the window on the 12th floor. As his screaming body hurtles towards the ground, he passes the 7th floor where a man shoots him with a 12-gauge shotgun, blowing most of his head off; who, my dear friends, is the murderer?"

The task this Guide undertakes is much more precise if one does not get all balled-up in the ill-fitting semantics usually associated with the issue.

The real question is this:

"Does a person have the legal right and the moral authority to take action to end his life in order to avoid future pain and suffering?"

I am the last person who needs to be preaching what is right and wrong from a religious or moral point of view. If you are a Believer, then you can study the Bible verses which mention suicide; however, I don't think the Bible speaks directly to the question which is before us.

In general terms, as far as I can tell, the Bible is a guide showing us how we should live. It calls for us to be proactive, to change the world for the better, not to simply sit back and endure all bad things as if we were mushrooms. Do we have a duty, as Christians, to relieve pain and suffering when we have the chance? Must we simply tolerate any and all of the bad things in this world?

For example, are we obligated to bend over and drop our drawers when we see a bully walking down the street in our direction? Of course not!

Who in his right mind will not attempt to duck if he sees a baseball flying towards his face, or at least turn his back to lessen the injury? We take all kinds of medicine in order to stop the hurt; no one suggests that we bear pain if we can avoid it. We wear safety belts in cars, not to avoid a wreck, but to reduce the seriousness of the injuries we might otherwise suffer if we have a wreck.

When I was a kid, my daddy had Hereford cattle. Once each year, we would round up the cattle, and separate the older calves from their Mamas, giving the Mamas a little time to recover before they dropped another calf.

To wean the calves, we would keep them locked in a big lot until they had gotten over their broken hearts, usually about a week. While the calves were locked up, a couple of farm hands would catch a bigger calf, tie a belly rope around his middle, and put me on his back. It was rodeo-time!

Always, always, always, Guy and Ray would tell me, "Don't forget to tuck your head when you hit the ground, and roll, roll, roll!"

Getting thrown off was a foregone conclusion; the only thing I could do was to prepare for the crash landing which was undeniably about to happen as your body is being sent skyward by a frightened 500-pound steer. I knew it was going to hurt when I hit the ground, but I did everything in my power to minimize my pain.

Boxing, perhaps the most brutal of all sports, does not require a contender to be beaten into oblivion by his opponent. The loser's side can toss in the towel at any time to stop the fight, and the referee is trained to intervene just as soon as one man is vanquished. Even our military leaders know the value of retreating in order to avoid insufferable losses when there is no reasonable hope of victory over the enemy. Surrender is also acceptable to avoid unnecessary loss of life.

From our earliest memory, our parents, our teachers, our peers, our coaches, EVERYBODY, tries to teach us how to avoid injury, pain, and death, but when it comes to the final act of dying, we are suddenly supposed to cowboy-up, and take it like a man?

Turning to the legal side of the issue, it's extremely difficult to prosecute a dead person who has successfully committed suicide. Accordingly, most states passed laws making it a crime to attempt suicide, or to assist someone else who has killed himself.

It is illegal in Georgia to assist a person who commits suicide. The law states:

"Any person with actual knowledge that a person intends to commit suicide who knowingly and willfully assists such person in the commission of such person's suicide shall be guilty of a felony and, upon conviction thereof, shall be punished by imprisonment for not less than one nor more than ten years."

Compare that with the basic tenets involved in the "Right to Die" or "Death with Dignity" statutes which a number of states have adopted. For example, Oregon's law:

*The Death with Dignity Act **(DWDA) allows terminally ill Oregon residents to obtain and use prescriptions from their physicians for self-administered, lethal medications.** Under the Act, ending one's life in accordance with the law does not constitute suicide.*

In Georgia, a physician who gives a lethal dose of medicine to a patient whom he knows is planning to use the medicine to kill himself, has committed a crime. In Oregon, the very same conduct is not a crime.

So, which way is the wind blowing?

When I was a kid, I could usually tell where North, South, East and West were. If I wanted to know the direction of the wind, I would lick my finger and hold it up in the air. The coolest side of my finger would be the side the breeze was coming from.

To understand which way the wind is blowing in terms of legal changes, and perhaps changes in society's attitudes, consider the following. The status quo in the United States back in the 1950's can be summarized as follows: A seriously ill person was treated with all due vigor, to get him well or to extend his life. It was the default setting, and doctors were expected to exert heroic efforts to keep the person alive as long as possible. But attitudes started changing a little at the time.

*In 1976, California passed the Natural Death Act which was the nation's first "aid in dying" statute which recognized living wills (legal documents which contained the dying person's end of life preferences), and the law also protected physicians who failed or refused to treat incurable illnesses.

This was the first legal attempt to recognize a patient's right to have some input as to his medical treatment, and to protect the physician who took a step back at the request of the patient.

*By 1984, Advanced Care Directives (similar to living wills) were recognized in 22 states and the District of Columbia.

*In 1990, Congress passes the Patient Self-Determination Act requiring hospitals to tell their patients they have the right to demand or refuse treatment. It's hard to imagine that it took a federal statute to establish that a patient has some control over the medical care being administered to his body.

*By 1994, all states recognized some type of advance directive.

It had taken 20 years before all the states had finally given legal recognition to the patient's right to make choices regarding his medical care. Hard on the heels of this development was the situation where the patient was asking for help to exercise his choices; usually asking a physician for assistance with dying.

The focus of the debate shifted to how much assistance could a physician give to a person who wanted to die.

*From 1994 to 2006, numerous cases were heard in federal court concerning the legality of state statutes commonly referred to as "Death with Dignity" and "Right to Die" laws. Finally, in 2006, the U.S. Supreme Court held Oregon's physician-assisted suicide law to be constitutional.

*By 2008, 341 terminal patients had used Oregon's Death with Dignity statute to accelerate the end of their lives.

*2012 The State of Georgia's highest court unanimously struck down the state's law prohibiting assisted suicide. Later the statute would be rewritten in a watered-down form.

*By 2018 Eight states have passed Death with Dignity laws, allowing physicians to assist the patient.

*By 2021, most states have either recognized the right a patient has to receive a doctor's assistance with dying, or the states have chosen not to enforce anti-suicide laws, or, finally, they have carved enough exceptions into those laws to make prosecution untenable.

What gives lawmakers, judges, bureaucrats, pencil-pushers, a hospital administrator, a doctor, or even family members the right to dictate and control the circumstances of a person's death? We are a "self-oriented" society, and rightly so, and it is our right to self-determine to the extent possible.

The legal arguments in support of patients' rights have run the gamut from equal protection to due process to rights of privacy. I was struck by the comments of Chief Justice Kogan way back in 1997 in a Florida Supreme Court decision. Chief Justice Kogan was outvoted as he tried to protect Floridians' right to die; in his lone dissenting opinion he wrote:

"What possible interest does society have in saving life when there is nothing of life to save but a final convulsion of agony? The state has no business in this arena. When his (the dying patient) pain becomes unbearable, which one of us on this Court will be at his bedside telling him to be brave and bear it?"

Most of us are proud Americans who recognize the privilege we have in this country to self-govern. Democracy, itself, is defined as independence, self-government, self-determination, self-legislation, self-rule, home rule, sovereignty and autonomy. What could be more fundamental than a citizen having the right, if he chooses, to avoid a painful, dismal death?

While drafting this guide, I had conversations with several friends and acquaintances about ending life to avoid pain and suffering. One religious friend told me he considered suicide to be a sin; but not an "unforgiveable sin". In essence, he would do it, and he wished it could have been done to save his mother so much pain and suffering several years ago. He would do it, then pray for forgiveness.

It's simply hard for me to grasp a concept whereby doing the right thing is still a sinful act.

Another friend told me when he could no longer bear to see his mother suffer, he secretly conspired with a nurse to "end her suffering." After one failed attempt, he was told by the nurse, "she will definitely be going to Heaven tonight," and she did.

It is time for good people all across this country to engage in open, frank and meaningful debate about the rights a dying person has, or should have. If one person has the right to demand extreme medical measures be employed to prolong his life, why shouldn't another person have the right in his final days to enlist medical science to terminate his unbearable pain and suffering?

It is my contention that a person has the legal right and the moral authority to have a say, if the opportunity arises, as to the method, manner and circumstances of his death. Relatively few people in the history of mankind have been granted such an opportunity. It would be a crying shame to let it go to waste.

A dying husband asked his wife: "Honey our 6th child looks different from our other 5 children. Did he have a different father?"

"I am sorry but yes"

"Can you tell me who?"

Wife: "Yes, you."

Husband died.

CHAPTER NINE

This is not rocket science.

Over 600,000 Americans are expected to die of cancer in 2021. Many of those patients will have Advanced Medical Directives giving some guidance to their family and medical providers with regard to issues that will almost certainly arise during the last stages.

One of the most popular provisions reads as follows:

(7B) _____ (Initials) Allow my natural death to occur. I do not want any medications, machines, or other medical procedures that in reasonable medical judgment could keep me alive but cannot cure me. I do not want to receive nutrition or fluids by tube or other medical means except as needed to provide pain medication.

This is about as far as the average person who attempts to take care of business goes with directions about how he is to be cared for and attended to during his final weeks, days, and hours. This simple directive in no way begins to address all the things to come.

The American Cancer Society has published a lengthy article entitled, "Nearing the End of Life". The article is intended to be a primer for a cancer patient and the patient's family, with the idea of helping them prepare for the sad, difficult days ahead.

What I found interesting about this article is not the advice that was given, but the forewarning of all the things the patient and his family could quite possibly suffer through, in this, the saddest of times. The Society's intent was to give a "heads-up," so the patient and family can prepare ahead of time, but the unintended consequence of the article is to motivate the patient to look for better ways to die.

First, there is the healthcare plan that has to be put together. This could mean weeks or even months in the hospital or in hospice care. Where, when, who, what, and how much is it going to cost? Hospice care at home can be even more of a challenge.

This is not a solo journey, but being pulled along on this heart-breaking trip is the spouse, the family, friends, and a host of medical providers and caretakers.

Every person's situation is different, but in every case, it is a time of high emotions. The Society warns that not only are there physical obstacles to deal with, but also the emotions, coming in from every angle which affect everyone. Fear, anger, guilt and regret, grief, feeling alone, anxiety and depression, confusion - the whole range of human emotions can be at play.

Today, as I am writing this chapter, a Facebook friend calls out to her friends to pray for her much-loved, and widely-respected father:

"Please say a prayer for Daddy this morning that he finds peace...the disease has not only affected the body, but the mind of the kindest, most loving, generous and compassionate man...Peace in his remaining years, months, weeks, days, moments...Peace, please Lord, is all we ask!"

I know this family; I've known her daddy all of my life. This is a close, four-generation family, and I can hear the hearts breaking from 20 miles away.

The referenced article offers suggestions about how to help the patient deal with the pain, the side effects from the medication, the patient's fatigue and weakness, loss of appetite, weight-loss, problems breathing, changes in bodily functions such as waste elimination, changes in consciousness, changes in metabolism, secretion, blood circulation, temperature, and the list goes on and on.

What this article describes is a slow-motion horror story starring a loved one as the helpless victim, with his family and friends being forced to witness his destruction, piece by piece. The process can go on for weeks, or months, or longer. The suggestions offered to ameliorate the situation are of little consolation; it is just too much. It is just too much to put anyone through, especially when there is a much better alternative.

Several years ago, I had the unpleasant experience of visiting the hospital where a distant relative lay dying. He had signed a medical directive, and had elected the provision above-listed, indicating he did not want fluids, nutrition, a ventilator, or any other machines. He wanted "death with dignity."

I stayed in his hospital room as long as I could take it; eventually, I had to leave. I was convinced then, and I am convinced now, I was witnessing his lungs fill with fluid, and he was drowning just a few feet away from me. There was absolutely nothing I could do, and as per his instructions, nothing the nurses could do either. I left the hospital only to learn a few hours later he had suffered a heart attack and died. I still believe the stress of choking to death together with a lack of oxygen caused his heart to explode.

If he was able to comprehend what was happening to him with his family only a few feet away, his last hours on Earth had to be the most awful hours of his entire life.

Why must a good man drown in his own fluids, struggling for each breath, or be stressed to the point of a heart attack before he is allowed to die? Why must he endure terrific pain and discomfort, lie helpless for days or weeks while one vital organ after the other fails? Whatever this is, it is not 'death with dignity.'

The worst criminals in our society are allowed their last meal, whatever food they want within reason. They are given time with family, and with a spiritual adviser if desired. They take a shower, put on fresh clothes, and are placed on clean, crisp linens. They are given the opportunity to say whatever they want to say to an assembled group of their closest family members and friends, and then a medical professional injects a lethal dose into their bloodstream which causes immediate, pain-free death; they are simply put to sleep.

Many years ago, I was County Attorney in my hometown. Animal shelters were just beginning to be a "thing" about that time. The County Commissioners did not want to spend a lot of money euthanizing stray dogs, so a couple of bright-eyed county employees built a gas chamber.

They would put the dogs in the sealed room, back a truck up near the structure, and connect a hose from the exhaust pipe of the truck running inside the room. Within a few minutes, with the truck idling, the dogs were dead from carbon monoxide.

The employees were very excited to demonstrate

their invention to members of the grand jury when they made their next inspection. To the horror of some of the grand jury members, they were suddenly unwitting witnesses to the gassing of several dogs.

The biggest recommendation the Grand Jury made to the County Commissioners in their Report was for the county to immediately cease gassing the dogs, and appropriate the necessary funds to euthanize the dogs by lethal injection.

It is incomprehensible that we take extraordinary, humanitarian steps to terminate a serial killer's life, as well as the lives of stray dogs, but then in the next breath, we have a great reluctance to allow a terminally-ill lady to choose to end her life in a dignified, painless, and controlled manner.

It is a commonly accepted practice to have a pet euthanized when he becomes terminally ill, when there is no realistic hope of recovery or improvement. The owner, out of love and compassion, makes an appointment with the Vet to have the animal put to sleep. Why? To avoid the pain and suffering that is bound to occur as the animal's condition deteriorates. It is the humane thing to do, and almost an act of cruelty not to euthanize the pet. Why, then, don't we do the humane thing for humans?

While I am a strong supporter of the right to die, it is not my intention to persuade or even to recommend that you end your life in any particular manner. My job is to let you know there are options out there, and to encourage you to consider those options in order to make the end-of-life decision with which you are the most comfortable.

If you are a senior citizen, you have already seen many

examples of old or sick people going through the process of dying; you already have your own stories. If you are interested in exploring the right to die, there are tons of groups, books, websites, Facebook pages, and other resources available for you to independently investigate all the pros and cons.

The purpose of this guide is not to fill in all of the blanks, not an A to Z treatise, but I like to think of it as a loud crack from a starting pistol. It is the beginning, the opening bell, the first round, the first inn . . . well, you get my drift.

Below is a short list of resources to help you get started. Please note the inclusion of HOPE which is an organization that opposes euthanasia.

Group Facebook Page "The Right to Die with Dignity and Compassion"
Exit International
"The Inevitable; dispatches on the right to die" by Katie Engelhart
HOPE, preventing Euthanasia and assisted suicide
www.Compassionandchoices.org

Me and my wife decided to form a suicide pact...

Weird thing was, that after she killed herself, I didn't

feel like dying anymore.

CHAPTER TEN

Eli's Coming!

Someone once said, "the only constant in life, is change."

Forty years ago, fewer than 10 percent of Americans chose to be cremated. Now, cremations are more popular than burials, over 50 percent, and the trend in favor of cremation continues.

The traditional religious teaching that man was made in the image of God, and therefore the body should not be destroyed, but should be adorned, preserved, and buried, has given way to a less ceremonious, and more efficient way of disposing of a dead carcass.

Two hundred years from now, 23rd century Americans will marvel at us primitive Americans who believed in spending a small fortune to bury a body in the ground, and wonder why we euthanized stray dogs, but allowed our beloved parents to suffer unmercifully for weeks before they were finally overtaken and beat down by death.

But Eli's coming!

As of this writing, nine states and the District of Columbia have legalized assisted suicide, also known as medical-aid-in-dying, MAID. They are:

California, Colorado, Hawaii, Maine, Montana, New Jersey, Oregon, Vermont and Washington.

At least 9 countries have legalized assisted suicide in one form or another; some have had laws on their books for decades. Those countries are Canada, Colombia, Belgium, Spain, Finland, Germany, Luxembourg, The Netherlands, Switzerland, and parts of Australia.

All of this legalization across the globe has come within the last 30 years, and in the United States, within the last 15 years. But hold on to your horses!

The Catholic news agency filed a report on February 9, 2021, that seven states currently have bills filed in the state legislatures attempting to legalize some form of assisted suicide. Those states are: Arizona, Indiana, Iowa, Kansas, New Mexico, New York, and North Dakota.

Indiana's bill includes a provision prohibiting a life insurance company from denying death benefits if a person should die following the guidelines provided in the proposed law. Iowa describes its pending bill as including "a palliative care option," basically renaming assisted suicide. That's an interesting twist, because all physicians are under a duty to provide palliative care to a dying patient.

Palliative care is sometimes defined as care given to improve the quality of life of patients who have a serious or life-threatening disease, such as cancer. Palliative care is an approach to care that addresses the person as a whole, not just their disease.

While all states do not have assisted suicide laws in place, it is clearly only a matter of time before assistance with dying will be legal across our Nation. The provisions of most of these state laws are almost identical:

1) The person must be an adult who is legally competent, and who knowingly and voluntarily makes the decision to receive assistance with dying.

2) The person must be a legal resident of the state in which he seeks assistance.

3) The person must provide the opinion of a medical doctor that he has less than six months of life expectancy.

4) The person must administer the lethal dose himself (some states allow a physician to administer it, if the person is not physically able to do so).

5) There are usually other safeguards built into most laws, such as waiting periods and mandatory counselling.

You won't find a lot of information about "Death with Dignity" laws, or "Right to Die" statutes, unless of course, you go looking. Then -oh boy-information from many sources is just bursting at the seams to get out.

There is an excellent, and exhaustive article available online from
www.deathwithdignity.org/learn/access/ entitled "How Death with Dignity Laws Work". Here are some of the highpoints:

a. You should make your decision while you are healthy; at a minimum, after you have thoroughly schooled yourself on all aspects of the law, when your ability to make medical decisions is unchallenged, and when you are able to articulate rational, unemotional reasons why you wish to access medical assistance with dying.

b. Even more important than convincing your loved ones, is persuading your primary care physician to support your decision. Most statutes require medical certification that you are mentally competent and emotionally stable before you can qualify. Your primary care physician will be the Doc first questioned, and the one with the strongest influence.

If your physician is not onboard, then it is time to change physicians, and find one who will support your decision, instead of sabotaging it. Assessing the level of support or resistance is critical, and you will need time to find a doctor who will be able and willing to assist when the time comes. If you don't do this ahead of time, and wait until the last minute, you may run out of time before you get too sick to complete the process.

A key step is to make sure the doctor documents in your medical records the fact that you wish to access a medical assisted dying program. This will be a part of your permanent records, and shows your wishes while you are still healthy, and possibly years before a terminal condition arises.

c. In most states, you will be required to present medical evidence that you have been diagnosed with a terminal illness that will "with reasonable medical judgment" lead to death within six months.

This requirement can prove to be difficult to satisfy. Your doctor may not want to commit to any time frame. Also, many doctors will not predict life expectancy for a person suffering from any form of dementia. As we know, Alzheimer's is "the long good-bye" with a person being alive, but severely impaired, for years. If your condition falls within a gray area as to life expectancy, you want a doctor who will support your efforts.

    d. While a number of states have "Right to Die" statutes, and more are in the pipeline, many states do not have these laws enacted as of now. If your state does not give you that right, then moving to another state might be required.

All state statutes require the person to be a resident of that state. Normally, there is no waiting period; you simply must be able to show you presently are residing in that state. The burden of proof of residency is on you, and some states even dictate the necessary documents which must be produced to proof residency. Others do not give a specific list.

Here are some documents you might need in order to satisfy the residency requirement:

Deed showing ownership of a home within the state, or a residential rental agreement.

State driving license, hunting license, voter registration card.

Bank account records showing local address; utility, telephone, and other public service accounts showing residence.

> e. There are several waiting periods, a second physician must corroborate the findings of the first physician, more than one request has to be made for the deadly prescription, and more waiting periods. In essence, the law provides mandatory breaks throughout the process to thwart any impulsive action.

Currently, there are so many hoops to go through that a terminally-ill person whose condition is deteriorating rapidly will probably die before he can finish the process UNLESS he has laid the groundwork to support his decision well in advance.

Right to Die statutes are under constant pressure to be less restrictive. There are groups who wish to eliminate the requirement that the person provide medical opinions indicating death will occur within six months.

Other groups are saying that the Right to Die must not exclude persons with mental disabilities.

Most statutes say the person himself must ingest the lethal dose, while others provide that a physician or licensed medical professional can administer the drug if requested.

Outside of the United States, Switzerland seems to be the place with the easiest rules to follow. Switzerland has long allowed both euthanasia and assisted suicide. It is the only country in the world which allows non-residents to visit the country and obtain assistance in dying while there. In fact, the phrase, "suicide tourism" is commonly used in Switzerland because people from all over the world come to Switzerland to end their life.

One of the biggest differences between the Swiss approach and the approach taken in the US, is that there does not have to be any medical opinion that death will likely occur within six months. As we all know, some extremely painful and debilitating processes can go on for years, and time of death is just a guess, causing most doctors to refuse to go on record with an opinion.

One of the biggest taboos in Switzerland is for anyone to make a profit by assisting in another's death. To profit from assisting someone to die is a crime. Rendering aid in these circumstances is seen more as an act of compassion and a civic duty.

The main purpose of this Guide is not to give you a "How to do it" method for obtaining aid in dying, but to let you know the changes in public opinion around the world, as well as here in the States, towards the notion of assisted suicide. Not only are opinions changing, but laws are changing, and rights of citizens are being recognized with rules and regulations being established to ensure that a righteous process is put into place.

IN CONCLUSION

A nursing home filled with people in pain, physically helpless, mentally-wrecked, or medicated into a state of permanent stupor, is a dreadful way to exit this otherwise wonderful life. It is not only terrible for the patient, but for anyone else who loves and cares for the hapless victim.

Every effort should be made to live as long as there is any quality of life; and the premise of this guide, is that quality of life can be maintained much longer in the person's home. Ironically, it is usually less expensive to render medical and non-medical aid to a disabled person in that person's home than to provide care 24/7 to a person confined in a nursing home.

In many cases, the quality of life evaporates weeks, months and even years before a person's body dies. Often times, those empty shells of once-beautiful, thriving people, have little choice but to suffer and waste away until death finally claims them.

The notion that a person should be able to choose the medical care he receives has taken hold around the world. The patient can choose to reject medical treatment, refuse medicine, and, now, finally, is being given permission under stringent circumstances to use medicine to end his suffering. Decades from now, our ancestors will be wondering what took us so long to reach such a logical conclusion.

Death is the ultimate personal experience. A person should, if possible, be able to exert some measure of control over that experience, rather than to subject it to some of society's old bad habits.

I challenge you to plan your old age, and to plan your farewell party. It's such an obvious thing to do.

A man sits at the deathbed of his mother-in-law.
She suffers very much and cries in agony:
"Oh I'm dying!" "It hurts!" "I'm gonna die soon!"
She stops for a few seconds and says:
"Well at least the weather is nice today."

The man says: "Hey dear, don't get distracted!"

"No Nursing Home for Me!"

By G. Keith Murphy

BOOKS BY THIS AUTHOR

Whoa Yonder!

Tomfoolery And Tragedy

Where Long Beards Grow

Stories From A Route Four Man

Made in the USA
Columbia, SC
01 September 2024

40799671R10054